Digging Up the Past

# LUCY SKELETON

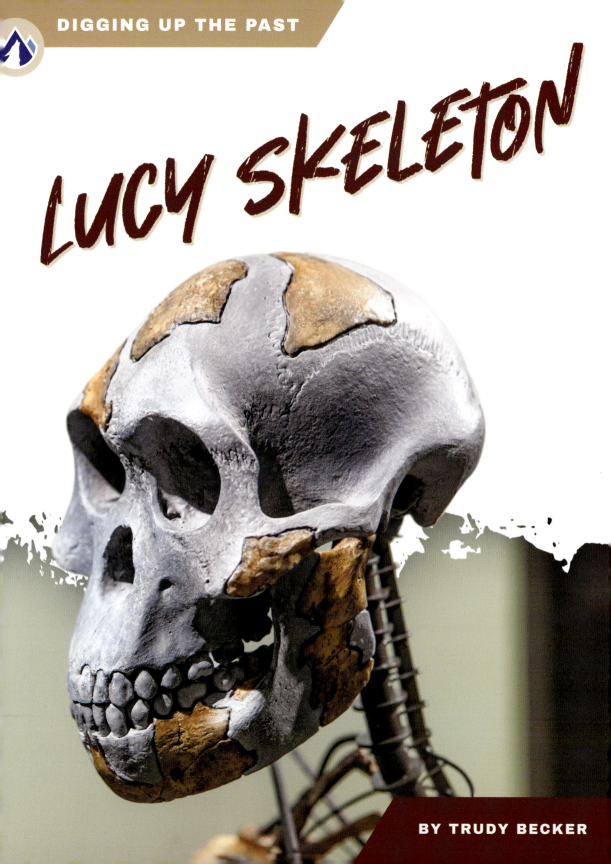

BY TRUDY BECKER

**WWW.APEXEDITIONS.COM**

Copyright © 2026 by Apex Editions, Mendota Heights, MN 55120. All rights reserved. No part of this book may be reproduced or utilized in any form or by any means without written permission from the publisher.

Apex is distributed by North Star Editions:
sales@northstareditions.com | 888-417-0195

Produced for Apex by Red Line Editorial.

Photographs ©: Kevin Fujii/Houston Chronicle/AP Images, cover; Shutterstock Images, 1, 4–5, 8, 10–11, 13, 14, 18, 22–23, 27; Bettmann/Getty Images, 6–7; Alain Nogues/Sygma/Getty Images, 9; Tom McHugh/Science Source, 16–17; Roman Uchytel/Science Source, 18–19, 29; Pat Sullivan/AP Images, 20; Clement Philippe/Arterra Picture Library/Alamy, 24–25; Sabena Jane Blackbird/Alamy, 26

Library of Congress Control Number: 2025930922

**ISBN**
979-8-89250-533-8 (hardcover)
979-8-89250-569-7 (paperback)
979-8-89250-639-7 (ebook pdf)
979-8-89250-605-2 (hosted ebook)

Printed in the United States of America
Mankato, MN
082025

**NOTE TO PARENTS AND EDUCATORS**
Apex books are designed to build literacy skills in striving readers. Exciting, high-interest content attracts and holds readers' attention. The text is carefully leveled to allow students to achieve success quickly. Additional features, such as bolded glossary words for difficult terms, help build comprehension.

# TABLE OF CONTENTS

**CHAPTER 1**
## DOWN IN THE DIRT 4

**CHAPTER 2**
## WHO IS LUCY? 10

**CHAPTER 3**
## SKELETON SECRETS 16

**CHAPTER 4**
## LEARNING FROM LUCY 22

COMPREHENSION QUESTIONS • 28
GLOSSARY • 30
TO LEARN MORE • 31
ABOUT THE AUTHOR • 31
INDEX • 32

**CHAPTER 1**

# DOWN IN THE DIRT

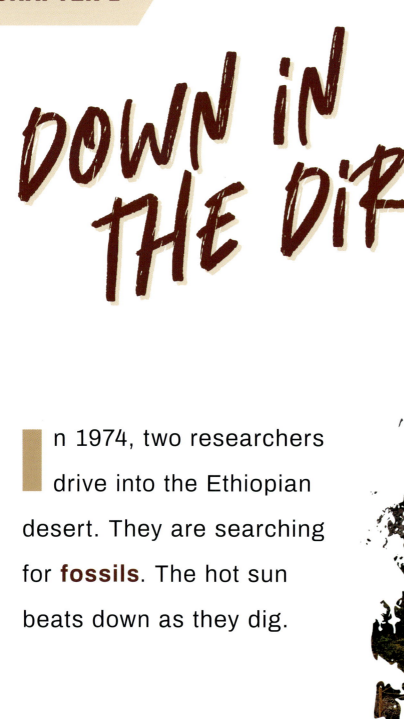

In 1974, two researchers drive into the Ethiopian desert. They are searching for **fossils**. The hot sun beats down as they dig.

Ethiopia is a country in eastern Africa. Much of its land is rocky and dry.

Donald Johanson was one of the researchers at the Ethiopia site. He found the first bone.

The researchers work all morning. Then they head back to the car for a break. Suddenly, one man spots something on the ground. He looks closer. It's a bone!

## PAST PEOPLE

Many researchers study human history. Some study a time even further back. They try to find fossils from very long ago. They want to learn how humans **evolved**.

When digging for fossils, researchers may use tools to break rocks or brush away dirt.

The researchers find more fossils nearby. For two weeks, they continue searching. Then the researchers put the fossil pieces together. They form a **partial** skeleton.

FAST FACT
The fossils made up 40 percent of a full body.

Researchers found hundreds of bone pieces. Some large bones had broken apart into small bits.

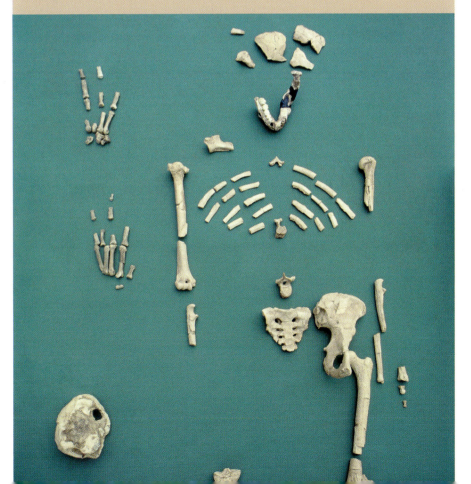

**CHAPTER 2**

# WHO IS LUCY?

The Lucy skeleton is a set of 47 fossilized bones. Scientists found them near Hadar, Ethiopia. The site had no **duplicate** bones. So, scientists knew they all came from the same body.

Scientists used Lucy's bone pieces to guess what the rest of her skeleton looked like.

The bones are very old. They come from a time before humans. Lucy was a different **species** of **hominin**.

## LUCY'S NAME

After finding the bones, researchers celebrated. They sang "Lucy in the Sky with Diamonds" by the Beatles. That's where Lucy's name comes from. In Ethiopia, she's called Dinkinesh. That means "you are marvelous."

Lucy's species was one of several types of hominins that lived before humans. ▶

The bones helped scientists learn about Lucy's species. She stood 3.5 feet (107 cm) tall. And she weighed around 60 pounds (27 kg).

**FAST FACT**
Lucy likely had wide cheekbones and a short forehead.

◀ **Researchers made copies of Lucy's bones. People study them or see them in museums.**

CHAPTER 3

# SKELETON SECRETS

**R**esearchers examined Lucy's skeleton. They studied the **pelvis** and teeth. They learned that Lucy was an adult female.

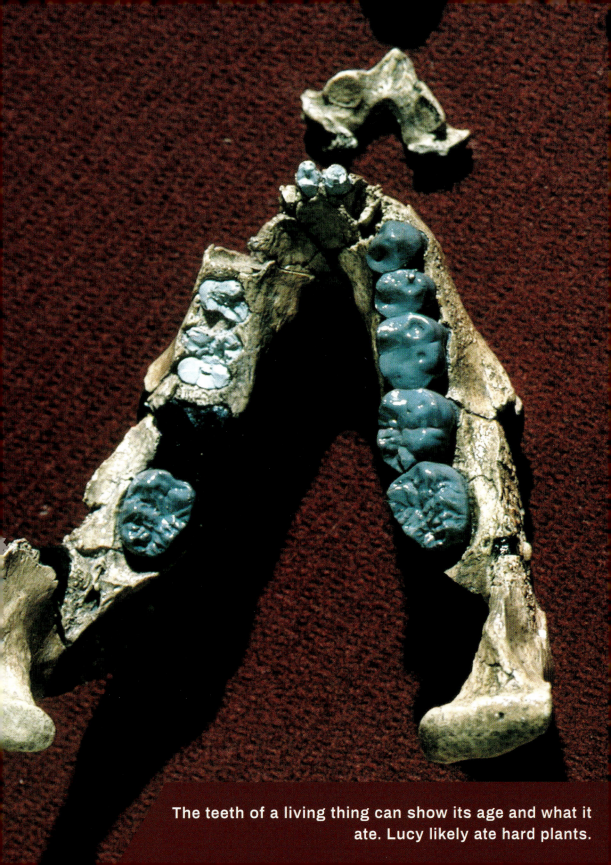

The teeth of a living thing can show its age and what it ate. Lucy likely ate hard plants.

Ash was trapped in rock around the same time as Lucy's fossils were.

Scientists also took ash from the discovery site. They tested this ash. It helped them learn how old Lucy's skeleton was. They think she lived nearly 3.2 million years ago.

**FAST FACT**
Lucy lived in a time called the Pliocene. Giant ground sloths and woolly mammoths lived then.

During the Pliocene, a type of large bear lived in Africa.

Lucy helped scientists study the link between humans and other apes. Her skeleton had some human-like **traits**. She had traits from non-human apes, too.

### BUILDING LUCY

Scientists took scans of Lucy's body. The scans showed many details. The scientists used this information to build computer models. The models showed what she may have looked like.

◀ Most scientists think Lucy's body was covered in hair.

CHAPTER 4

# LEARNING FROM LUCY

Researchers had found early hominin bones before. But Lucy was a different species. She was older than other finds. And her skeleton was one of the most complete.

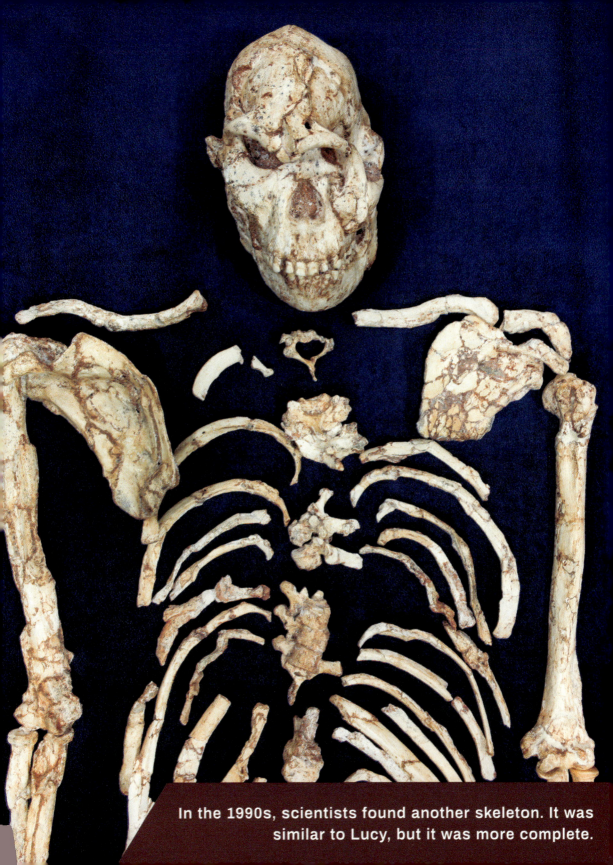

In the 1990s, scientists found another skeleton. It was similar to Lucy, but it was more complete.

Researchers study each hominin skeleton's traits. Then they compare the skeletons' ages. This helps them learn how traits changed as hominins evolved.

**FAST FACT**
Researchers have found more than 20 different species of hominins.

People have found hominin fossils in several African countries. These include South Africa, Tanzania, and Kenya.

 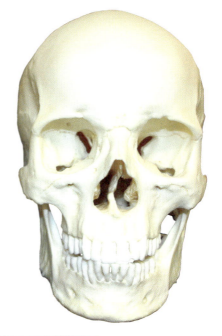

Lucy's skull (left) is smaller than a human skull (right).

For example, Lucy had long arms. So, she likely climbed trees. But she walked on two legs. Her brain was bigger than other apes' but smaller than a human's. These things helped scientists understand the link between her and humans.

## BROKEN BONES

Researchers took X-rays of Lucy's bones. Her right arm was hurt. Some scientists think this injury came from falling out of a tree. This fall may have killed her.

Lucy's bones are kept in a museum in Ethiopia. Scientists built a safe to protect them.

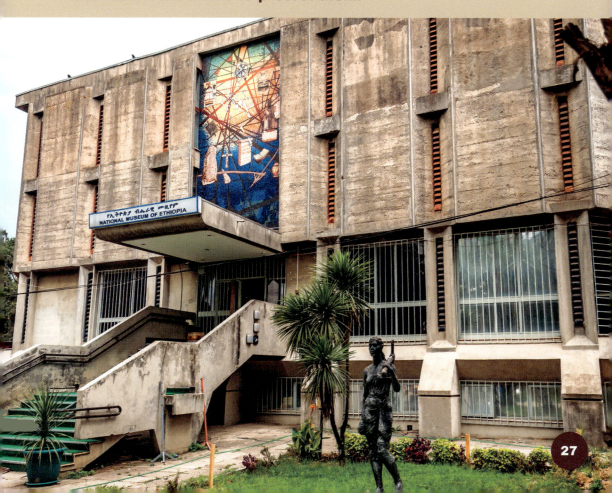

# COMPREHENSION QUESTIONS

Write your answers on a separate piece of paper.

1. Write a few sentences explaining the main ideas of Chapter 2.

2. What would you like to learn about life on Earth 3.2 million years ago?

3. Where was Lucy found?
   - A. Ethiopia
   - B. South Africa
   - C. England

4. How would comparing the ages of skeletons show how hominin traits changed?
   - A. Newer skeletons would all have the same traits.
   - B. Older skeletons would show which traits came first.
   - C. Older skeletons would not be studied.

**5.** What does **examined** mean in this book?

*Researchers **examined** Lucy's skeleton. They studied the pelvis and teeth. They learned that Lucy was an adult female.*

  **A.** threw away
  **B.** looked closely at
  **C.** broke apart

**6.** What does **injury** mean in this book?

*Her right arm was hurt. Some scientists think this **injury** came from falling out of a tree.*

  **A.** harm to a person's body
  **B.** healing a person's body
  **C.** cooking a person food

Answer key on page 32.

# GLOSSARY

**duplicate**

Exactly the same as something else.

**evolved**

Went through a series of many changes, usually over a long time, and became a new species as a result.

**fossils**

Remains of plants and animals that lived long ago.

**hominin**

A group of modern humans and older human-like species.

**partial**

Not complete.

**pelvis**

The set of bones that connect the chest and spine to the legs. It includes the hip bones.

**species**

A group of animals or plants that are similar and can breed with one another.

**traits**

Details that set a creature apart from others.

## BOOKS

Murray, Julie. *Ötzi the Iceman*. Abdo Publishing, 2022.

Neuenfeldt, Elizabeth. *Woolly Mammoths*. Bellwether Media, 2025.

Storm, Rebecca. *Fossil Investigators*. Lerner Publications, 2025.

## ONLINE RESOURCES

Visit **www.apexeditions.com** to find links and resources related to this title.

## ABOUT THE AUTHOR

Trudy Becker lives in Minneapolis, Minnesota. She likes exploring new places and loves anything involving books.

# INDEX

## A
apes, 21, 26
ash, 18

## B
Beatles, 12

## D
Dinkinesh, 12

## F
fossils, 4, 7–9, 10

## H
Hadar, Ethiopia, 4, 10, 12
hominins, 12, 22, 24–25
humans, 7, 12, 21, 26

## P
Pliocene, 19

## S
species, 12, 15, 22, 25

## T
traits, 21, 24

## X
X-rays, 27

**ANSWER KEY:**
1. Answers will vary; 2. Answers will vary; 3. A; 4. B; 5. B; 6. A